Amazing Biomes

OCEANS

BROWN BEAR BOOKS

Published by Brown Bear Books Ltd

4877 N. Circulo Bujia
Tucson, AZ 85718
USA

and

First Floor
9-17 St. Albans Place
London N1 0NX

© 2015 Brown Bear Books Ltd

ISBN: 978-1-78121-243-1

Library of Congress Cataloging-in-Publication Data
available upon request

Author: Leon Gray
Designer: Karen Perry
Picture Researcher: Clare Newman
Editor: Tim Harris
Children's Publisher: Anne O'Daly
Design Manager: Keith Davis
Editorial Director: Lindsey Lowe

Manufactured in the United States of America

CPSIA compliance information: Batch# AG/5567

Picture Credits

The photographs in this book are used by permission
and through the courtesy of:

T=Top, C=Center, B=Bottom, L=Left, R=Right

Front cover: ©William Bradberry/Shutterstock.
Interior: 1, ©Igor Zh/Shutterstock; 2-3, ©Neamov/
Shutterstock; 4b, ©Mogens Trolle/Shutterstock;
4-5, ©Brian Kinney/Shutterstock; 6tl, ©Tatiana Ivkovich/
Shutterstock; 6bl, ©Photoaeye/Shutterstock;
7tr, ©Outdoorsman/Shutterstock; 7cr, ©Mogens
Trolle/Shutterstock; 7bl, ©BMJ/Shutterstock;
8-9, ©Bruno Ismael Silva Alves/Shutterstock;
9, ©Studio Art/Shutterstock; 10-11, ©CB Pix/
Shutterstock; 11tr, ©Photo Researchers/FLPA;
12b, ©Distinctive Images/Shutterstock;
12-13, ©Alexander Sher/iStock/Thinkstock;
13br, ©Neonja/Richard Barte/Wikipedia;
14, ©Fomengto/Shutterstock; 15t, ©Ethan Daniels/
Shutterstock; 15b, ©Francis Abbott/Nature PL/Alamy;
16, ©Isabelle Kvehn/Shutterstock; 16-17, ©Alterfalter/
Shutterstock; 18-19, ©Igor Zh/Shutterstock;
19tr, ©Laura D/Shutterstock; 20tr, ©John A. Anderson/
Shutterstock; 20b, ©Andrea Izzotti/Shutterstock;
21, ©Boris Pamikov/Shutterstock; 22, ©Matt 9122/
Shutterstock; 23t, ©Rich Carey/Shutterstock;
23b, ©Photo Researchers/FLPA; 24, ©Nigel Pavitt/AWL
Images/Getty Images; 25t, ©Antoni Halim/Shutterstock;
25b, ©Trubavin/Shutterstock; 26-27, ©Tony Moran/
Shutterstock; 27t, ©Jeffrey Rotman/Corbis;
28cl, ©Mogens Trolle/Shutterstock; 28cr, ©Isabelle
Kvehn/Shutterstock; 28br, ©Ethan Daniels/Shutterstock;
28-29, ©Brian Kinney/Shutterstock; 29cl, ©Trubavin/
Shutterstock; 29bl, ©Jeffrey Rotman/Corbis.

Brown Bear Books has made every attempt to contact
the copyright holder. If you have any information
please contact licensing@brownbearbooks.co.uk

All other photographs and artworks © Brown Bear Books Ltd.

Contents

INTRODUCTION

Oceans cover more than two-thirds of our planet's surface. All oceans contain salty water. They are home to a huge variety of animals and plants.

Biomes are places where animals and plants live and grow. Some prefer dry deserts, while others live in tropical rain forests. The animals and plants that live in the world's oceans have **adapted** to live in salty water. Some animals and plants live near the surface of the water. Others are found far beneath the waves in the murky ocean depths.

Read on to find out what oceans are like—and how plants, animals, and people live in and around them.

Gray whales live in the Pacific Ocean. They feed close to the ocean surface.

CORALS

Corals may look like plants, but they are animals. Corals live on the seafloor in warm, tropical water. Often, many corals grow together to form a coral reef. Many fish feed near the reefs.

OCEANS OF THE

This map shows the world's five oceans. The darker blue areas are the deepest parts of the oceans. The Pacific is the world's biggest ocean.

An orca, or killer whale, leaps from the water in the Pacific Ocean. This behavior is called breaching.

A trawler returns to port after fishing for herring in the Atlantic Ocean off the coast of Canada.

NORTH AMERICA

ATLANTIC OCEAN

PACIFIC OCEAN

SOUTH AMERICA

SOUTHERN OCEAN

ANTARCTICA

WORLD

OCEAN

Walruses rest on sea ice floating on the Arctic Ocean. These **mammals** dive beneath the surface of the water to hunt fish.

ARCTIC OCEAN

EUROPE

ASIA

AFRICA

INDIAN OCEAN

AUSTRALIA

A great white shark hunts for squid in the Indian Ocean.

An emperor penguin jumps onto sea ice in the Southern Ocean.

CLIMATE AND

WATER WAVES

Wind blows over the surface of the ocean and creates waves. When very big waves crash onto the shore, spray blows inland.

The water that makes up the world's oceans is constantly on the move. It plays a big part in shaping Earth's weather. Oceans also have their own underwater zones, which change as you go deeper beneath the surface.

ZONES

Warm and cold water flows around the oceans in currents. The wind and the spinning movement of Earth in space combine to create these currents. A warm current called the Gulf Stream flows from tropical parts of the Atlantic Ocean. It reaches as far north as the coast of Britain. Wind that blows over the Gulf Stream also becomes warm. So does the land that the wind blows over. In this way, the temperature of the ocean changes the climate of the land nearby.

When there is little or no wind, the surface of the ocean may seem flat and still, but currents keep the water on the move below.

Ocean Zones

There are three main ocean zones between the surface of the water and the seafloor. The top zone is called the **sunlight zone** because it is bathed in sunlight during the day. Most ocean animals and plants live in the sunlight zone. As you sink deeper into the **twilight zone**, the light fades, the water gets cooler, and the **water pressure** increases. The **midnight zone** is at the bottom of the ocean depths. This is a world of total darkness. Few animals and no plants can survive in this extreme environment.

A blacktip reef shark swims near a shoal of small fish in the sunlight zone of the Indian Ocean.

DEEP FISH

In 2014, a **shoal** of 17 fish was found in a very deep part of the midnight zone in the Pacific Ocean. Thought to be snailfish, the fish were 26,700 feet (8,145 meters) below the surface.

The hatchetfish lives in the midnight zone of the world's oceans.

PLANTS

Most of the ocean's plant life consists of algae. Most algae drift in ocean currents and provide food for sea creatures. Other plants live in coastal regions, where the ocean meets the land.

Most algae that live in the ocean are tiny. They can only be seen under a **microscope**. Algae are not true plants. They do not have roots, stems, and leaves like plants that grow on the land. Like plants, algae need sunlight to grow. They can grow on the ocean shore and in the top 660 feet (200 meters) of the ocean. Light does not reach any deeper than that, so algae cannot grow there.

The seaweed that washes up on beaches is a type of algae. People collect seaweed to eat. The green or brown fronds look like the leaves of plants that grow on land.

Plankton

Millions of tiny **organisms** drift around in the sunlight zone at the top of the ocean. They are called plankton. Some are plantlike algae, such as the one in the photo to the right (magnified by 1,000). Others are microscopic animals. Plankton is very important. Many sea creatures, from fish to whales, depend on plankton for their food.

True Plants

Seagrasses are the only flowering plants that live under the ocean. They grow best in clear, shallow waters. Seagrasses produce flowers, fruit, and seeds just like plants on land. They form large meadows on the ocean floor. Many sea creatures rely on them for food.

Other plants, such as mangrove trees, live along the coast, where the sea meets the land. The trunks, branches, and leaves grow in forests above the water while most of the roots are submerged.

BIO FACT

Mangrove forests are home to many animals. Shellfish cling to the roots, fish breed in the shallow water around the roots, and birds nest in the treetops.

Trees on Stilts

Mangrove trees look like they are growing on stilts. The "stilts" are special roots that anchor the tree in the mud and prop it above the water. These roots filter out salt from the seawater. Mangrove trees store the salt in their leaves. After a while, the trees get rid of the excess salt by shedding some of their leaves.

Neptune grass grows on the ocean floor in the Mediterranean Sea. One colony near the Spanish island of Ibiza is more than 100,000 years old.

ANIMALS

You can find different animals in every part of the ocean, from the surface all the way down to the seafloor. Some animals spend all of their lives under the water. Others use the oceans to hunt or mate but live mostly on the land.

- Green sea turtles use
- their enormous flippers
- like paddles to swim
quickly through
the water.

Green Sea Turtle

Sea turtles live in the warm waters of the Atlantic, Pacific, and Indian oceans. Male green sea turtles never leave the water. Females come ashore every two years to lay their eggs. These turtles can hold their breath for hours as they swim underwater looking for food. Young turtles eat crabs and jellyfish, but adults are **vegetarians**.

In shallow waters, crabs and starfish roam across the seafloor. In some tropical waters, corals grow in huge reefs. These reefs provide shelter for other animals, such as anemones, eels, reef sharks, and urchins. Farther out to sea, large fish, turtles, and whales swim in the open ocean in search of food. Some animals, such as anglerfish and tube worms, have even adapted to life in the murky ocean depths.

SHOAL OF FISH

In a single group, or shoal, of sardines, there may be thousands of fish. When the shoal changes direction, every fish moves at exactly the same time.

Sea Mammals

Sea mammals are similar to land mammals. They all have warm blood and breathe air into their lungs. But sea mammals are adapted to life in the water. They have a thick layer of fat to keep them warm in the cold seawater. They can hold their breath for some time underwater, but they also need to rise to the surface to breathe. Common sea mammals include dolphins, dugongs, and seals.

FOOD CHAIN

In some places, cool ocean currents bring **nutrients** to the surface. Plankton feed on these nutrients. Fish eat the plankton, and dolphins and whales eat the fish.

Dorsal fin

Flipper

Bottlenose dolphins leap out of the water as they swim through the open ocean. Bottlenose dolphins live in groups, or pods, with up to 30 members. They hunt fish, shrimp, and squid in the top layer of the ocean.

Remora fish follow the dugong as it feeds

Beak is shaped like a bottle

Ocean Herbivores

On the land, **herbivores** such as cattle, sheep, wildebeest, and zebras graze on grasslands. In the ocean, swimming herbivores called dugongs graze on seagrasses and algae on the ocean floor. For this reason, dugongs are sometimes called "sea cows." These sea mammals live in tropical parts of the Indian and Pacific oceans. They can hold their breath for up to six minutes while they feed.

19

Life on the Ocean Floor

In places where the ocean is shallow, the ocean floor may have coral reefs, mudflats, and rocky and sandy areas. But the ocean floor is usually much deeper, thousands of feet below the surface. Animals adapt to life in these places in different ways. Some, such as flatfish, live just under the seabed. Others, such as anemones, attach themselves to coral reefs. Deep-sea animals, such as tube worms, live in total darkness and under extreme water pressure.

FISH FOOD

Copepods are some of the most common animals in the world. These tiny animals look like mini shrimp. If copepods did not exist, many fish in the ocean would go hungry!

A giant octopus uses its tentacles to feel its way across the seabed. This octopus eats fish, including small sharks.

Colorful Hunter

Some animals creep along the ocean floor in search of food. They include colorful **predators** called sea slugs. They eat other animals, including other sea slugs. Some have **toxins** in their bodies that harm any animal that eats them. A sea slug's bright colors warn other animals that it is dangerous to eat them.

- Giant clams float in the water when they are young. When they become adults, they settle on the seabed and stay there.

Top Predators

The ocean's top predators sit at the very top of the food chain. They are animals that no other animals hunt for food. Top ocean predators include fearsome fish, such as sharks, and also sea mammals, such as blue whales—the world's biggest animal. Perhaps the deadliest of all sea predators is the killer whale. These intelligent animals hunt in packs. Killer whales will eat almost anything they can catch, from fish and squid to seals, sea lions, and other whales. They have even been known to attack great white sharks.

A hammerhead shark's eyes are at the end of stalks that stick out on either side of its head. The shark can see above and below itself at all times.

Dorsal fin helps shark change direction

Eye

Mouth

Eye can see up and down

REEF HUNTER

Reef sharks swim near coral reefs and hunt fish and squid. These sharks are agile swimmers. They can twist and turn at great speeds.

Deep Predators

Fangfish live in the murky ocean depths, 9,200 feet (2,800 meters) beneath the surface. Light cannot reach this far, so fangfish live in the dark. However, these fish can make their own light, called **bioluminescence**. The fangfish switch off this body light when they are hunting so that their **prey** cannot see them.

PEOPLE

People have a strong bond with the oceans. The water provides a source of food, including seaweed, fish, and shellfish. People use ships to carry themselves and their goods across the world.

FISH FOOD

A fisherman waits to spear a fish in the shallow waters of Lake Turkana, Kenya. This is an ancient method of fishing.

People have always relied on the oceans for survival. Traditional fishing techniques use spears, small nets, or rods to catch fish. For some, this is still the only way they can feed their families. Today, fishing is also a huge industry. In fact, so many fish are caught in fishing nets that some, such as cod, are in danger of being wiped out. Before trains, cars, and planes were invented, the oceans were the best way for people to travel around the world. They first used simple wooden rafts, then sailing ships. Modern cargo ships are powered by engines and carry food, clothes, and other goods from country to country.

Huge ships called supertankers carry oil thousands of miles across the world's oceans.

Ocean Fun

Today, one of the most popular uses of the ocean is for water sports, such as diving, sailing, swimming, and surfing. Every year, many families go to beach resorts on their vacations. There they can relax together and enjoy these leisure pursuits.

THE FUTURE

The world's oceans are a valuable resource. People have to work together to protect them from harmful pollution and overfishing.

In the last 100 years, the oceans have come under serious threat. People have taken large amounts of valuable resources from the sea, such as fish and oil. Human activities have also created problems, such as pollution, **climate change,** and **global warming**.

WIND FARMS

Most electricity we use comes from burning fossil fuels. This creates pollution. Wind farms are a cleaner way to generate electricity. They use the energy of the wind instead.

Scientists explore the ocean depths in submersibles. They study the oceans in order to help protect them.

Rising Sea Levels

If Earth's temperature continues to rise due to global warming, polar ice will melt. Sea levels will rise, and many islands will disappear. At the same time, pollution is destroying ocean biomes such as coral reefs. Many sea creatures are dying out. Countries around the world now recognize these problems. They are working together to protect the oceans, so that future generations of people can enjoy them.

QUIZ

Try this quiz to test your knowledge of ocean biomes. You can find the answers on page 31.

1 This is a gray whale. Which of the world's oceans does it live in?

2 Green sea turtles spend almost all their lives at sea. Why do females sometimes come ashore?

3 What type of seaweed can be found growing in huge forests from the ocean floor?

4 Can you name three other popular water sports apart from surfing?

Fact File

○ The world's oceans cover more than two-thirds of Earth's surface area.

○ There are five main oceans—the Pacific, Atlantic, Indian, Arctic, and Southern oceans.

○ The three main ocean zones are called the sunlight, twilight, and midnight zones.

○ The most common plant life in the ocean are plantlike algae, such as seaweed.

5 This vehicle is used to explore the ocean depths. What is it called?

Winners and Losers

⬆ Some gulls have learned to feed on garbage dumps. They have more food to give their chicks and can raise larger families.

⬇ Hammerhead sharks could die out because so many are being fished for food.

⬇ The number of sea turtles in the oceans is falling. People hunt them and eat their eggs. Many turtles are also caught in fishing nets.

GLOSSARY

adapted: When an animal or plant has slowly changed to fit in with its surroundings.

bioluminescence: The process of producing light from inside the bodies of living things. Some deep-sea fish use bioluminescence to trap prey and send signals to other deep-sea fish.

biomes: The places where animals and plants usually live and grow.

climate change: The warming of Earth's climate produced by the increase in greenhouse gases in the atmosphere.

currents: The movement of cool and warm water beneath the surface of the ocean.

food chain: The order in which animals feed on plants and other animals within a biome.

global warming: The gradual increase in Earth's temperature caused by human activities, such as burning fossil fuels.

herbivores: Animals that eat only plants.

mammals: Animals with warm blood that breathe air using lungs. Mammals feed their young on milk produced by the mammary glands.

microscope: An instrument that people use to see extremely small objects, such as plankton.

midnight zone: The zone at the bottom of the ocean. The midnight zone is in complete darkness.

nutrient: A substance that provides energy to an organism.

organisms: A scientific word to describe any living thing, such as an animal or plant.

predators: Animals that hunt and eat other animals.

prey: Animals that are hunted by other animals, called predators.

shoal: A large group of fish.

sunlight zone: The zone at the very top of the ocean. The sunlight zone is bathed in sunlight during the day.

toxins: Any substances produced by animals and plants that can harm other living things.

twilight zone: An ocean zone that lies between the sunlight zone and the midnight zone.

vegetarians: Animals that do not eat the bodies of other animals.

water pressure: The weight of water that pushes down on things in the ocean.

FURTHER RESOURCES

Books

Calver, Paul and Toby Reynolds. *Visual Explorers: Ocean Life.* Hauppauge, NY: Barron's, 2014.

Hague, Bradley. *Alien Deep: Revealing the Mysterious Living World at the Bottom of the Ocean.* Washington, DC: National Geographic, 2012.

Macquity, Miranda. *Ocean* (DK Eyewitness). New York: Dorling Kindersley, 2014.

Rizzo, Johanna. *Oceans: Dolphins, Sharks, Penguins, and More!* Washington, DC: National Geographic Children's Books, 2010.

Websites

NASA's Climate Kids
climatekids.nasa.gov/menu/ocean
NASA's "Eyes on the Earth" website includes lots of information on oceans and what we can do to protect them.

National Geographic: Ocean
oceans.nationalgeographic.com/ocean/ocean-life
Learn about the world's oceans and the amazing animals and plants that live in them. Includes breathtaking photos and videos, plus news on climate change.

Smithsonian Ocean Portal
ocean.si.edu
Check out incredible facts about ocean life and ecosystems, such as giant squid and coral, as well as the seafloor, ancient seas, and marine fossils.

World Wide Fund for Nature: Oceans
www.worldwildlife.org/habitats/oceans
Discover awesome species of ocean animals and plants via colorful photos and videos, and find out about conservation plans for ocean biomes.

Answers to the quiz: **1** Pacific Ocean. **2** To lay their eggs. **3** Kelp. **4** Diving, sailing, and swimming. **5** A submersible.

INDEX